A Note From Rick Renner

I am on a personal quest to see a "revival of the Bible" so people can establish their lives on a firm foundation that will stand strong and endure the test when the end-time storm winds begin to intensify.

In order to experience a revival of the Bible in your personal life, it is important to take time each day to read, receive, and apply its truths to your life. James tells us that if we will continue in the perfect law of liberty — refusing to be forgetful hearers but determined to be doers — we will be blessed in our ways. As you watch or listen to the programs in this series and work through this corresponding study guide, I trust that you will search the Scriptures and allow the Holy Spirit to help you hear something new from God's Word that applies specifically to your life. I encourage you to be a doer of the Word that He reveals to you. Whatever the cost, I assure you — it will be worth it.

> Thy words were found, and I did eat them;
> and thy word was unto me the joy and rejoicing of mine heart:
> for I am called by thy name, O Lord God of hosts.
> — Jeremiah 15:16

Your brother and friend in Jesus Christ,

Rick Renner

Accepting Your God-Assigned Place

Copyright © 2020 by Rick Renner
8316 E. 73rd St.
Tulsa, Oklahoma 74133

Published by Rick Renner Ministries
www.renner.org

ISBN 13: 978-1-68031-678-0

eBook ISBN 13: 978-1-68031-683-4

How To Use This Study Guide

This five-lesson study guide corresponds to *"Accepting Your God-Assigned Place" With Rick Renner* (**Renner TV**). Each lesson in this study guide covers a topic that is addressed during the program series, with questions and references supplied to draw you deeper into your own private study of the Scriptures on this subject.

To derive the most benefit from this study guide, consider the following:

First, watch or listen to the program prior to working through the corresponding lesson in this guide. (Programs can also be viewed at **renner.org** by clicking on the Media/Archives links.)

Second, take the time to look up the scriptures included in each lesson. Prayerfully consider their application to your own life.

Third, use a journal or notebook to make note of your answers to each lesson's Study Questions and Practical Application challenges.

Fourth, invest specific time in prayer and in the Word of God to consult with the Holy Spirit. Write down the scriptures or insights He reveals to you about being filled with the Spirit and empowered by Him in your daily life.

Finally, take action! Whatever the Lord tells you to do according to His Word, do it.

For added insights on this subject, it is recommended that you obtain Rick Renner's book *The Point of No Return: Tackling Your Next New Assignment With Courage and Common Sense*. You may also select from Rick's other available resources by placing your order at **renner.org** or by calling 1-800-742-5593.

TOPIC

Getting Into Alignment With God's Will for Your Life

SCRIPTURES

1. **Acts 9:15** — ...For he is a chosen vessel unto me, to bear my name before the Gentiles, and kings, and the children of Israel.

2. **Acts 26:13-18** — At midday, O king, I saw in the way a light from heaven, above the brightness of the sun, shining round about me and them which journeyed with me. And when we were all fallen to the earth, I heard a voice speaking unto me, and saying in the Hebrew tongue, Saul, Saul, why persecutest thou me? it is hard for thee to kick against the pricks. And I said, Who art thou, Lord? And he said, I am Jesus whom thou persecutest. But rise, and stand upon thy feet: for I have appeared unto thee for this purpose, to make thee a minister and a witness both of these things which thou hast seen, and of those things in the which I will appear unto thee; delivering thee from the people, and from the Gentiles, unto whom now I send thee, to open their eyes, and to turn them from darkness to light, and from the power of Satan unto God, that they may receive forgiveness of sins, and inheritance among them which are sanctified by faith that is in me.

3. **Romans 11:13** — For I speak to you Gentiles, inasmuch as I am the apostle of the Gentiles, I magnify mine office.

4. **Galatians 2:8** — For he that wrought effectually in Peter to the apostleship of the circumcision, the same was mighty in me toward the Gentiles.

5. **Ephesians 3:1** — For this cause I Paul, the prisoner of Jesus Christ for you Gentiles.

6. **Acts 18:1,2** — After these things Paul departed from Athens, and came to Corinth; And found a certain Jew named Aquila, born in Pontus, lately come from Italy, with his wife Priscilla; (because that Claudius had commanded all Jews to depart from Rome:) and came unto them.

GREEK WORDS

1. "found" — εὑρίσκω (*heurisko*): pictures a moment when one makes a surprising discovery; carries an element of surprise; it is where we get the word "eureka"

SYNOPSIS

The five lessons in this study on *Accepting Your God-Assigned Place* will focus on the following topics:

- Getting Into Alignment With God's Will for Your Life
- Do Not Veer From What God Has Called You To Do
- When Your Ways Please the Lord, Even Your Enemies Will Be at Peace With You
- Embracing Your God-Given Place
- Be the Best You Can Be at Whatever God Has Called You To Do

The emphasis of this lesson:

Like the apostle Paul, God has a specific place designed and assigned just for you. Getting into alignment with His plan is not always instantaneous. Many times it is a process. But once you're in line with His will for your life, powerful things begin to take place.

Did you know that God has a specific place designed just for you? It is a tailor-made position in which He wants to shine forth His amazing grace through you and transform the lives of others. Of course, discovering God's will for your life and actually getting into it is often not instantaneous. It is a process that takes time. A careful study of the Old and New Testament clearly reveals this.

Think about Abraham. He heard God's call on his life while he was still in Mesopotamia (*see* Acts 7:2,3), but it took him several years to get his will into alignment with God's will. Then there was Moses. He was saved from death as an infant and raised in Pharaoh's palace. He had a desire in his heart to deliver his people from slavery, but it took 40 years of preparation out in the desert before he stepped into his God-assigned place.

If it has been difficult for you to get into alignment with what God has asked you to do, you are not alone. Nevertheless, when you fully embrace your God-assigned place and begin to function in it, you will leave the black-and-white world of monotony and enter the full-color world that is fully alive and energized by God's grace!

Paul's Call Was Difficult for Him To Grasp

In the New Testament, one of the greatest examples demonstrating the process of *knowing God's will* and *being in His will* is seen in the life of the apostle Paul. From the moment he encountered the Spirit of Christ on the road to Damascus, God's will for his life was made known to him. But it took him time to fully embrace it.

The Bible tells us that God spoke to Ananias, a follower of Christ living in the city of Damascus, and instructed him to go and pray for Paul (whose name was still Saul at this point). Acts 9:15 says, "But the Lord said unto him, Go thy way: for he [Paul] is a chosen vessel unto me, to bear my name before the Gentiles, and kings, and the children of Israel."

In this passage, the Holy Spirit declared Paul's threefold, God-assigned place. First and foremost, he was to bear Christ's Name before the Gentiles; this was his most important calling. Second, he was to be a witness for Christ before kings. Third and least of all, he was to bring the Gospel to the children of Israel — the Jews. This was God's divine order for Paul's life.

Although he had clearly heard what God said, it was a very hard assignment to accept. Think about it — Paul was a Jew to the core of his being. He said he was "circumcised the eighth day, of the stock of Israel, of the tribe of Benjamin, an Hebrew of the Hebrews; as touching the law, a Pharisee" (Philippians 3:5). Having been raised in the rigidity of Judaism, Paul had been taught from the youngest age that Gentiles were like "dogs," and he was to steer clear of them. Thus, when God told Paul that his primary call was to the Gentiles, it was hard for him to stomach.

Paul Recounted His Conversion and His Call to King Agrippa

In Acts 26, we find Paul toward the end of his life standing before King Agrippa, recounting the day of his conversion to Christ. He began by saying, "At midday, O king, I saw in the way a light from heaven, above the brightness of the sun, shining round about me and them which journeyed with me. And when we were all fallen to the earth, I heard a voice speaking unto me, and saying in the Hebrew tongue, Saul, Saul, why persecutest thou me? it is hard for thee to kick against the pricks" (Acts 26:13,14).

Isn't it interesting that when Paul heard the voice from Heaven speaking to him, it was in his native, Hebrew tongue? This indicates that when God speaks to people, He speaks to each individual in their own language — using words and phrases he or she will clearly understand. He is extremely personal and wants us to understand what He is saying.

In verse 15, Paul answered and said, "…Who art thou, Lord? And he said, I am Jesus whom thou persecutest." In that moment, Paul became a Christian. Romans 10:13 confirms this declaring, "For whosoever shall call upon the name of the Lord shall be saved." Paul called Jesus "Lord" and was saved right then and there. The Holy Spirit entered his life, and he was born again.

The Spirit of Christ answered Paul and said, "Rise, and stand upon thy feet: for I have appeared unto thee for this purpose, to make thee a minister and a witness both of these things which thou hast seen, and of those things in the which I will appear unto thee" (Acts 26:16).

Amazingly, right from the start, Jesus made known to Paul the purpose for his life. The truth is, the moment you were born again and the Holy Spirit came into you, you have had possession of God's will for your life. It is not floating around somewhere in the universe. It was deposited inside of you, in seed form, at salvation. According to this verse, Paul was to be a witness of the supernatural revelations he had seen and a minister of the things he would see in the future.

Furthermore, the Lord said He would be "delivering [Paul] from the people, and from the Gentiles, unto whom now I send thee" (Acts 26:17). The words "send thee" is a translation of the Greek word *apostolo*, which is from where we get the words *apostle* and *apostolic*. Hence, Jesus told Paul that he was going to be an *apostle* to the Gentiles. Verse 18 says, "To open their eyes, and to turn them from darkness to light, and from the power of Satan unto God, that they may receive forgiveness of sins, and inheritance among them which are sanctified by faith that is in me."

Paul's Call to the Gentiles Was Clear to Him

Again and again, Scripture reveals that Paul knew his primary call was to the Gentiles. He wrote:

> **For I speak to you Gentiles, inasmuch as I am the apostle of the Gentiles, I magnify mine office (Romans 11:13).**

> **(For he that wrought effectually in Peter to the apostleship of the circumcision, the same was mighty in me toward the Gentiles.) (Galatians 2:8)**

> **For this cause I Paul, the prisoner of Jesus Christ for you Gentiles (Ephesians 3:1).**

Make no mistake — Paul knew he was called to Gentile ministry, and He knew it from the moment of his conversion. But as we said at the beginning of this lesson, knowing God's will and being in His will are two different things. It would take Paul some time to process what Christ had said to him and actually transition into his call.

Paul Was Fixated on Reaching the Jews

We know from Scripture that Paul was not readily accepted by the apostles in Jerusalem. In fact, his presence and activities caused such a ruckus, the church leaders put him on a boat in Caesarea and sent him back to his homeland of Tarsus (*see* Acts 9:30). It was Barnabas who went back to Tarsus to seek Paul (then called Saul) and bring him to Antioch to serve in leadership (*see* Acts 11:25,26).

It was while serving as a leader in Antioch that the Holy Spirit selected Paul and Barnabas to launch out on his first missionary journey (*see* Acts 13:2,3). Church history reveals that for the first five years of Paul's ministry, he consistently attempted to bring the Gospel to the Jews. He understood the Jews — he knew their language, their culture, and how they thought. Thus, because he was comfortable with them and deeply burdened for their salvation, his attention and efforts were fixed on his Jewish brothers.

In every town Paul went, he was magnetically drawn to the local synagogue where he reasoned and discussed the Scriptures with the Jews. In the cities of Salamis (Acts 13:5), Antioch (Acts 13:14), Iconium (Acts 14:1), Thessalonica (Acts 17:1), Berea (Acts 17:10), Athens (Acts

17:16,17), and even Corinth (Acts 18:1,4), the first place he went as soon as his feet hit the ground was the synagogue.

Unfortunately, because Paul had reversed the divine order of God's calling, he was met with much frustration, hardship, and failure the first five years of ministry. Instead of going to the Gentiles first, kings and leaders second, and the Jews last, he went to the Jews first and paid very little attention to the Gentiles. His life serves as an example of what can happen when our priorities are out of line. If we are not focused on what God has called us to do, we are going to experience much frustration and very little fruit just as Paul did.

Paul Recalibrated His Calling in Athens

A major turning point came during Paul's second missionary journey. As he made his way into the city of Athens, he went straight to the synagogue to dispute the Scriptures with the Jews as he had done so many times before. This time, however, he did something different. He also began sharing the Gospel with Gentile philosophers in the marketplace, and eventually they took him to the Areopagus on Mars Hill where he spoke almost exclusively to Gentiles. Their receptivity to the Gospel was quite remarkable, and there were even certain high-ranking Athenians who were saved.

Acts 18:1 says, "After these things Paul departed from Athens, and came to Corinth." Still alone, he journeyed about 50 miles on foot down the interior road between Athens and Corinth. This gave him ample time to think about all he had experienced in ministry up to that point. It's likely he thought about the strife and turmoil that the Jews had stirred up in virtually every city where he attempted to minister to them. Undoubtedly, he also thought about his most recent efforts in Athens and the unprecedented receptivity of the Gentiles. All these things and more he may have weighed carefully in his mind as he entered the city of Corinth.

A Snapshot of Corinth's History

Of all the cities on the face of the earth in the ancient world, none was more Gentile than Corinth. It had a reputation for being rowdy, riotous, and full of rebellion. As a matter of fact, it was so out of control that it was totally destroyed by Rome in 146 BC. About 100 years later, in 44 BC, Julius Caesar decided to rebuild Corinth. To entice people to lend a hand in its rebuilding, he offered special privileges and monetary bonuses to those who would come and resettle there.

The greatest number of people who accepted the emperor's offer was legionnaires, soldiers, and sailors. Thus, the city of Corinth was founded by a rough group of individuals whose language and behavior was exceedingly foul. Corinth became known as a city world-famous for its sinfulness and pagan practices. Moreover, because Julius Caesar believed he and his family were direct descendants of the Greek goddess Aphrodite (the Latin name was Venus), he decided to reconstruct Corinth and dedicate it to her.

Keep in mind, Corinth sat on an isthmus between northern and southern Greece, so a person traveling in that area would have to go through Corinth, whether he wanted to go east to west, west to east, south to north, or north to south. The city had two harbors — one that led straight to the Roman province of Asia and another to Italy. Great numbers of travelers and sailors entered in and out of Corinth's ports on a frequent basis, coming from all over the world to enjoy the city's pleasures of sex, sensuality, and an abundance of alcohol.

Corinth had its fair share of temples that were dedicated to pagan gods; including those to Apollo and Zeus, as well as a significant and historical one dedicated to the worship of Aphrodite, the goddess of sex. The Greeks in Corinth believed a multitude of various kinds of blessings came from her. Hence, Corinth became a huge brothel with a booming sex industry. It was so renowned for sexual perversity and free-flowing alcohol that even the pagans of Rome and other parts of the world used the nickname "Corinthian" to describe any person who lived a life of drunkenness and debauchery.

Paul Experienced a Paradigm Shift in Corinth

Paul's arrival in Corinth marked the dawn of a new day and a new way of doing ministry. As he first entered the town, the Bible says he, "...found a certain Jew named Aquila, born in Pontus, lately come from Italy, with his wife Priscilla; (because that Claudius had commanded all Jews to depart from Rome:) and came unto them" (Acts 18:2).

The word "found" in verse 2 is the Greek word *heurisko*, and it pictures *a moment when one makes a surprising discovery*. This word carries *an element of surprise*, and it is from where we get the word "eureka." As Paul made his way into Corinth, it must have been quite an unnerving experience. He was traveling by himself into a city that some have called the "gutter of society." But then surprisingly, out of the blue, he bumped into Aquila and Priscilla — a Christian couple from Rome whom he was immediately connected with in spirit.

Aquila and Priscilla had been forcefully evicted from their home and their home country. The Emperor Claudius had issued an edict to expel Jews from Rome — an imperial decree that impacted Jewish believers. We're not sure how the event unfolded, but this type of imperial edict was often carried out in an abrupt and harsh manner during early New Testament times. Thus, Aquila and Priscilla had begun traveling east — not by *choice*, but rather by *force*.

From their home in Rome, the two headed for the nearest port, where they boarded a ship that would ultimately take them to Corinth. When they finally arrived in the city, they must have felt defeated, discouraged, and dejected. But as these two walked the streets of this unfamiliar city, they just "happened" to meet the apostle Paul, who had just arrived in Corinth from Athens. Life for all three of them was about to change drastically.

Although Paul initially went to the synagogue in Corinth to reason with the Jews, it wasn't long until he redirected his energies to the Gentiles. At long last, he was putting his primary focus on the prophetic order that God had designed for his life. He had realigned himself with God's plan that was given to him when he first came to Christ.

As a result, First Corinthians 2 and Second Corinthians 12 tell us that signs, wonders, and mighty deeds followed Paul as he preached the Word to the Corinthian pagans! Plus, Paul found remarkable favor with multitudes of Gentiles who responded to his message, and as a result, he established a large, powerful church in the city of Corinth.

STUDY QUESTIONS

Study to shew thyself approved unto God, a workman that needeth not to be ashamed, rightly dividing the word of truth.
— 2 Timothy 2:15

1. What new insights did you learn about the ancient city of *Corinth* — its founding, location, what it was known for, etc.?

2. What did you discover about the apostle *Paul* that you had not known before? How about Paul's ministry companions — *Aquila and Priscilla?*

PRACTICAL APPLICATION

> But be ye doers of the word, and not hearers only,
> deceiving your own selves.
> —James 1:22

1. When Paul accepted Christ as his Lord and Savior on the road to Damascus, his God-assigned place was revealed to him. Do you know your God-assigned place in life — your divine calling? If so, briefly describe what you understand it to be.

2. According to Scripture, Paul's calling was threefold, but his *primary focus* was to be an apostle to the Gentiles. How about you? Is your calling multifaceted? What would you say is your *main calling* and your *secondary calling?* How are you making your main calling top priority?

3. If you do not know God's calling for your life — your God-assigned place — take time right now to pray, *"Lord, I humble myself before You and ask You to reveal to me my God-assigned place. What is my purpose and the calling on my life? Please make it clear to me. In Jesus' name."*

LESSON 2

TOPIC

Do Not Veer from What God Has Called You To Do

SCRIPTURES

1. **Acts 18:1,2** — After these things Paul departed from Athens, and came to Corinth; and found a certain Jew named Aquila, born in Pontus, lately come from Italy, with his wife Priscilla; (because that

Claudius had commanded all Jews to depart from Rome:) and came unto them.

2. **Acts 18:4-8** — And he reasoned in the synagogue every sabbath, and persuaded the Jews and the Greeks. And when Silas and Timotheus were come from Macedonia, Paul was pressed in the spirit, and testified to the Jews that Jesus was Christ. And when they [the Jews] opposed themselves, and blasphemed, he shook his raiment, and said unto them, Your blood be upon your own heads; I am clean: from henceforth I will go unto the Gentiles. And he departed thence, and entered into a certain man's house, named Justus, one that worshipped God, whose house joined hard to the synagogue. And Crispus, the chief ruler of the synagogue, believed on the Lord with all his house; and many of the Corinthians hearing believed, and were baptized.

GREEK WORDS

1. "found" — εὑρίσκω (*heurisko*): pictures a moment when one makes a surprising discovery; carries an element of surprise; it is where we get the word "eureka"

2. "reasoned" — διαλέγομαι (*dialegomai*): from διά (*dia*) and λέγω (*lego*); the word διά (*dia*) means through and carries the idea of something that is thorough; the word λέγω (*lego*) depicts speech; it means to thoroughly discuss; to discuss all the way through, from one side to the other; it pictures the exchanging of thoughts; the giving and receiving of information to reach deeper understanding; a going back and forth of thoughts and ideas

3. "persuaded" — πείθω (*peitho*): depicts persuasion; one who is convinced, coaxed, or swayed from one opinion to the opinion held by another; a person coaxed from a particular conviction to embrace a different one; a persuasion that leads to conviction and belief; absolute confidence; convinced to the core; rock-solid certainty

4. "the Jews" — Ἰουδαῖος (*Ioudaios*): Jews; Jewish by birth and by faith

5. "the Greeks" — Ἕλλην (*Hellen*): Greek; non-Jewish; pictures gentiles; pagans

6. "pressed" — συνέχω (*sunecho*): to be pressured or to be compelled

7. "opposed" — ἀντιτάσσομαι (*antitassomai*): a compound of ἀντί (*anti*) and τάσσω (*tasso*); the word ἀντί (*anti*) means against and implies hostility; the word τάσσω (*tasso*) means to set in order or to arrange; in history, it was a military term to denote the ordering of troops to

prepare for an attack against an enemy; compounded, depicts taking a hostile position to fight against in an orderly and premeditated fashion; nothing happenstance about this, as it depicts an orderly assault

8. "blasphemed" — βλασφημέω (*blasphemeo*): to slander; to accuse; to speak against; to speak derogatory words for the purpose of injuring or harming one's reputation; also signifies profane, foul, unclean language; can refer to blaspheming the divine, but in general, it is any derogatory speech intended to defame, injure, or harm another's reputation; includes any type of debasing, derogatory, nasty, shameful, ugly speech or behavior intended to humiliate someone

9. "shook" — ἐκτινάσσω (*ektinasso*): to shake violently; to wildly swing; to shake until something falls off

10. "I am clean" — καθαρὸς ἐγώ (*katharos ego*): the word καθαρὸς (*katharos*) means cleansed or pure; ἐγώ (*ego*) means "I"; compounded, the phrase is used here to mean, "I have finally gotten you out of my system"; "I am free of you; of your contamination"

11. "henceforth" — ἀπὸ τοῦ νῦν (*apo tou nun*): ἀπὸ (*apo*) implies a decisive separation; combined, these words mean from this moment or from this exact moment onward

12. "the Corinthians" — not the Jewish community, but the pagans of the city

SYNOPSIS

When you get where God wants you to be and begin doing what He has called you to do, there will always be something that comes up to try and get you to veer away from His will. Therefore, once you know your God-assigned place, you must learn to dig in your heels and choose not to budge from your spiritual post.

After years of struggling to fully align himself with God's will, the apostle Paul finally embraced his call to the Gentiles and began to experience great success in the city of Corinth. But when two of his close Jewish friends showed up, he felt pressured to turn away from his calling and refocus his attention on the Jews. When he did, he was immediately met with the same hostility and frustration he had experienced before. Without a second thought, he instantly did an about-face and returned to his God-assigned ministry to the Gentiles. Once again, God's peace, power, and protection came, and Paul never again veered from his calling.

The emphasis of this lesson:

Once you are aware of your God-assigned place in life, it is imperative that you do all you can not to veer from it. Don't let your friends talk you out of it or let the devil push you away from it. Hold tightly to God's divine calling.

We saw in our first lesson that God's primary call on the apostle Paul was to bring the Gospel to the Gentiles. But because he was a Jew through-and-through and intensely loved his Hebrew brethren, he found this mandate extremely difficult to fulfill. In fact, for the first five years of his ministry, the first place he went in every city he visited was the local synagogue to discuss the Scriptures and reason with the Jews. Sadly, his reversal of God's call on his life produced much frustration, heated friction, and very little fruit.

It wasn't until Paul arrived in the city of Corinth that he began to experience a real breakthrough in ministry. For the first time in his life he began to consciously redirect his energy and efforts toward the Gentiles. Surprisingly, in the midst of the darkest pagan environment, supernatural signs and wonders began to manifest in extraordinary ways. Paul was in the right place, doing the right thing with the right people, and he found great favor among the Gentiles.

Tragic Events Produced a Divine Connection

Acts 18:1 tells us, "After these things Paul departed from Athens, and came to Corinth." Although Athens was a city devoted to idolatry, the idolatry was sophisticated. Corinth, however, was like the gutter of the ancient world, and when Paul arrived there, he was alone. It must have been quite a shock for him to enter this city of such decadence and debauchery.

Remember, Corinth was world-famous for its sinfulness and pagan practices. At its founding, Julius Caesar had dedicated this city to Aphrodite, the goddess of sex. Corinth was so renowned for its immorality that even the pagans of Rome and other parts of the world used the nickname "Corinthian" to describe any person who lived a life of drunkenness and debauchery.

The Bible goes on to say that Paul "...found a certain Jew named Aquila, born in Pontus, lately come from Italy, with his wife Priscilla; (because that Claudius had commanded all Jews to depart from Rome:) and came unto them" (Acts 18:2). We saw that the word "found" is the Greek word *heurisko*, which depicts *a moment when one makes a surprising discovery*. It carries *an element of surprise* and is where we get the word "eureka."

The Emperor Claudius had issued an edict to expel all Jews from Rome — an imperial decree that impacted Jewish believers. One early Roman historian named Suetonius wrote that the reigning emperor had displaced Jews who "were constantly inciting tumults under their leader Christos." Apparently, the believers in Rome were preaching about Jesus and causing such a ruckus that the emperor could no longer stand it, so he evicted all the Jews.

It was a tragic turn of events when Aquila and Priscilla and others were forcefully ejected from their home because of religious persecution. We're not sure how the event unfolded, but this type of imperial edict was often carried out in an abrupt and harsh manner during early New Testament times. They very likely had no time to say goodbye to their families or fellow church members. They had been evicted from their home, isolated from Roman society, and ejected from their country. This was a huge loss for Aquila and Priscilla financially, mentally, emotionally, and socially.

Nonetheless, they traveled east from their home in Rome — not by choice, but rather by force. They headed for the nearest port, where they boarded a ship that would ultimately take them to Corinth. When they finally arrived in the city on the western side of Greece, they must have felt defeated and dejected. But as they walked the streets of this unfamiliar city, they just "happened" to meet the apostle Paul, who had just arrived in Corinth from Athens.

God is always working behind the scenes, and while He didn't arrange for Aquila and Priscilla to be evicted from their home, He masterfully took the situation and turned it into something monumentally good. When their lives intersected with Paul's life, a powerful supernatural partnership was birthed, and their lives would never again be the same.

Paul 'Reasoned' With and 'Persuaded' Jews *and* Greeks

From the time Paul arrived in Corinth, the Bible says "...he reasoned in the synagogue every sabbath, and persuaded the Jews and the Greeks"

(Acts 18:4). Notice carefully what was taking place. First, it says Paul "reasoned" in the synagogue. The word "reasoned" is the Greek word *dialegomai*, a compound of the words *dia* and *lego*. The word *dia* means *through* and carries *the idea of something that is thorough*. The word *lego* depicts *speech*. When the two words are compounded to form the new word *dialegomai*, it means *to thoroughly discuss; to discuss all the way through, from one side to the other*. It depicts *exchanging thoughts; the giving and receiving of information with someone to reach deeper understanding; a going back-and-forth of thoughts and ideas*.

The Bible also says Paul "persuaded," which is the Greek word *peitho*, and it describes *persuasion* or *one who is convinced, coaxed, or swayed from one opinion to the opinion held by another*. It depicts *a person coaxed from a particular conviction to embrace a different one; a persuasion that leads to conviction and belief*. This word can also be translated as *absolute confidence; convinced to the core; rock-solid certainty*.

Who was Paul *persuading* and with whom did he *reason?* The Bible says "the Jews *and* the Greeks" (Acts 18:4). The phrase "the Jews" in Greek is *Ioudaios*, which describes *Jews* or *Jewish by birth and by faith*. "The Greeks" is the Greek word *Hellen*, and it means *Greek; non-Jewish; gentile;* or *pagan*. Thus, Paul was not just speaking to Jews. He had finally thrown open the door to non-Jews, redirecting his ministry to the dark, deviant, twisted pagans.

This was a very important change in focus for Paul as he was now embracing his God-assigned place, fulfilling his primary calling. He was leading both Jews and Gentiles alike to Christ. He had found great favor among the Gentiles, and his ministry was beginning to thrive for the first time since he had left Antioch.

The Arrival of Silas and Timothy Pressured Paul

Then something happened. Acts 18:5 says, "And when Silas and Timotheus were come from Macedonia, Paul was pressed in the spirit, and testified to the Jews that Jesus was Christ." To understand this verse, we must look at the original Greek text, which shows that the words "in the spirit" do *not* appear in the most ancient manuscripts. It simply says, "… Paul was pressed…"

The word "pressed" is the Greek word *sunecho*, which means *to be pressured* or *to be compelled*; it carries the idea of *manipulation*. Up until that point,

Paul had been ministering side-by-side with Aquila and Priscilla, presenting the Gospel to Gentiles and Jews alike and having great success among the Gentiles. But when Silas and Timothy showed up, Paul felt "pressed" — *pressured, compelled, manipulated* — to go back to his old way of doing things; which was speaking to Jews only.

If you stop and think about it, you'll remember Silas and Timothy had traveled with Paul for years, and they were only accustomed to seeing Paul minister to Jews. In every town they went, they saw Paul go to the synagogue to reason with the Jews. Now, to see him totally focused on sharing the Gospel with the Gentiles was quite a shock to them.

It seems that the moment Silas and Timothy arrived they must have put pressure on Paul. Maybe they went to him and said, "What are you doing? Have you forgotten that you're a Jew? Have you forgotten the Gospel is to the Jew first? Why are you spending all your time and energy speaking to these Greek pagans? What has happened to you?" Clearly, when Silas and Timothy arrived, Paul felt pressed.

The Jews 'Opposed Themselves' and 'Blasphemed'

What happened when Paul turned back to the Jews and gave himself exclusively to witnessing to them? The Bible says, "And when they [the Jews] opposed themselves, and blasphemed, he [Paul] shook his raiment, and said unto them, Your blood be upon your own heads; I am clean: from henceforth I will go unto the Gentiles" (Acts 18:6).

First, it says the Jews "opposed" themselves. This is the Greek word *antitassomai*, which is a compound of the words *anti* and *tasso*. The word *anti* means *against* and implies *hostility*; the word *tasso* means *to set in order* or *to arrange*, and it was *a military term to denote the ordering of troops to prepare for an attack against an enemy*. When the words *anti* and *tasso* are compounded, the new word *antitassomai* depicts *taking a hostile position to fight against in an orderly and premeditated fashion*. In other words, there is nothing happenstance about this; it is *an orderly assault*.

The Bible also says the Jews "blasphemed," which in Greek is *blasphemeo*, meaning *to slander; to accuse; to speak against; to speak derogatory words for the purpose of injuring or harming one's reputation*. It also signifies *profane, foul, unclean language* and can refer to *blaspheming the divine*. In general, the word *blasphemeo* is *any derogatory speech intended to defame, injure, or harm another's reputation*; it includes *any type of debasing, derogatory, nasty, shameful, ugly speech or behavior intended to humiliate someone.*

The moment Paul turned his attention entirely on the Jews, they became hostile and attacked him with derogatory, defaming words against his character and used profane, blasphemous language.

Paul Made a Clean Break From His Past Pattern

The Scripture says when Paul saw their reaction, he "shook his raiment." The word "shook" in Greek is *ektinasso*, and it means *to shake violently; to wildly swing; to shake until something falls off.* This response by Paul was in obedience to what Jesus Himself said in the gospels: "And whosoever shall not receive you, nor hear you, when ye depart thence, shake off the dust under your feet for a testimony against them…" (Mark 6:11).

Paul's actions were an indictment against the Jews. In fact, he went on to say, "…Your blood be upon your own heads; I am clean: from henceforth I will go unto the Gentiles" (Acts 18:6). The phrase "I am clean" in Greek is *katharos ego.* The word *ego* means "I" and indicates Paul *emphatically drawing attention to himself.* The word *katharos* means *cleansed or pure.* Its use here is the equivalent of Paul saying, "I have finally gotten you out of my system; I am free of you — of your contamination."

After years of trying and trying and trying to reach the Jews and being brutally mistreated, Paul finally reached the point where he was done with it. He said, "…from henceforth I will go unto the Gentiles" (Acts 18:6). The word "henceforth" in Greek is *apo tou nun.* The word *apo* implies a *decisive separation; from this moment.* Paul declared *from that exact moment forward*, he would be going in a different direction.

Scripture goes on to say, "And he departed thence, and entered into a certain man's house, named Justus, one that worshipped God, whose house joined hard to the synagogue. And Crispus, the chief ruler of the synagogue, believed on the Lord with all his house; and many of the Corinthians hearing believed, and were baptized" (Acts 18:7,8).

This passage records a marked shift in the effectiveness of Paul's ministry. The moment he made the decision to redirect his energy and efforts to the Gentiles, suddenly, Crispus — who was the *chief ruler* or *archbishop* of the synagogue — surrendered his life to Jesus. Upon hearing this news, the Bible says many of "the Corinthians" also became Christians. "The

Corinthians" refers not to the Jewish community, but to *the pagans* of the city. Thus, when Paul got his priorities straight and began reaching out to the Gentiles Christ had called him to reach, a multitude in the city believed and were baptized.

Friend, if God has revealed His assigned place for you, the best thing you can do is surrender to His plan and ask Him for His grace to walk it out. When the enemy comes to distract or derail you, resist him and stay the course. If your family and friends try to sway you away from God's will, don't listen. If you will remain obedient and keep doing what you know in your heart God has called you to do, you will reap a harvest of abundant fruit just as Paul did.

STUDY QUESTIONS

> Study to shew thyself approved unto God, a workman that needeth
> not to be ashamed, rightly dividing the word of truth.
> — 2 Timothy 2:15

1. The fact that Paul quickly turned away from the Gentiles and turned back to the Jews when Silas and Timothy arrived is likely an indication that he was afraid of what they might think of him. What does Proverbs 29:25 say about *the fear of man*? Why must we ask God to deliver us from this common, but deadly trap? (Consider Jesus' words in John 12:42,43; Matthew 10:28-33.)

2. Take a moment to reflect on the time Paul opposed Peter in Galatians 2:11-13. Why do you think Paul acted this way? Where might he have learned this lesson he was trying to get across to Peter?

PRACTICAL APPLICATION

> But be ye doers of the word, and not hearers only,
> deceiving your own selves.
> — James 1:22

1. Imagine you were like Aquila or Priscilla — a former Jew who became a Christian living at the time when Claudius evicted all Jews from Rome. In light of all that this couple faced, what do you think would have been the hardest thing for you to deal with personally? Why?

2. The moment Paul called Jesus *Lord* on the road to Damascus, he was instantly born again. Can you recall the day when *you* invited Jesus to be Lord of your life? Briefly describe what took place. What touches your heart most deeply about your born-again experience?

3. Church history reveals that for the first five years of his ministry, Paul reversed God's calling on his life. Instead of taking the Gospel to the Gentiles first, Paul made the Jews his top priority. What was the result of his misplaced priorities? What does this say to you about God's calling on your life? Is *God's* top priority for your life *your* top priority? Is the "main thing" truly the main thing? What type of results have you been getting from your efforts?

LESSON 3

TOPIC

When Your Ways Please the Lord, Even Your Enemies Will Be at Peace With You

SCRIPTURES

1. **Proverbs 16:7** — When a man's ways please the Lord, he maketh even his enemies to be at peace with him.

2. **Acts 18:1,2** — After these things Paul departed from Athens, and came to Corinth; and found a certain Jew named Aquila, born in Pontus, lately come from Italy, with his wife Priscilla; (because that Claudius had commanded all Jews to depart from Rome:) and came unto them.

3. **Acts 18:4-18** — And he reasoned in the synagogue every sabbath, and persuaded the Jews and the Greeks. And when Silas and Timotheus were come from Macedonia, Paul was pressed in the spirit, and testified to the Jews that Jesus was Christ. And when they [the Jews] opposed themselves, and blasphemed, he shook his raiment, and said unto them, Your blood be upon your own heads; I am clean: from henceforth I will go unto the Gentiles. And he departed thence, and entered into a certain man's house, named Justus, one that worshipped

God, whose house joined hard to the synagogue. And Crispus, the chief ruler of the synagogue, believed on the Lord with all his house; and many of the Corinthians hearing believed, and were baptized. Then spake the Lord to Paul in the night by a vision, Be not afraid, but speak, and hold not thy peace: for I am with thee, and no man shall set on thee to hurt thee: for I have much people in this city. And he continued there a year and six months, teaching the word of God among them. And when Gallio was the deputy of Achaia, the Jews made insurrection with one accord against Paul, and brought him to the judgment seat, saying, This fellow persuadeth men to worship God contrary to the law. And when Paul was now about to open his mouth, Gallio said unto the Jews, If it were a matter of wrong or wicked lewdness, O ye Jews, reason would that I should bear with you: but if it be a question of words and names, and of your law, look ye to it; for I will be no judge of such matters. And he drave them from the judgment seat. Then all the Greeks took Sosthenes, the chief ruler of the synagogue, and beat him before the judgment seat. And Gallio cared for none of those things. And Paul after this tarried there yet a good while, and then took his leave of the brethren, and sailed thence into Syria, and with him Priscilla and Aquila...

4. **Isaiah 54:17** (*NLT*) — ...No weapon turned against you will succeed. You will silence every voice raised up to accuse you. These benefits are enjoyed by the servants of the Lord; their vindication will come from me. I, the Lord, have spoken!

5. **1 Corinthians 1:1** —Paul, called to be an apostle of Jesus Christ through the will of God, and Sosthenes our brother.

GREEK WORDS

1. "found" — εὑρίσκω (*heurisko*): pictures a moment when one makes a surprising discovery; carries an element of surprise; it is where we get the word "eureka"

2. "the Jews" — Ἰουδαῖος (*Ioudaios*): Jews; Jewish by birth and by faith

3. "the Greeks" — Ἕλλην (*Hellen*): Greek; non-Jewish; pictures gentiles; pagans

4. "pressed" — συνέχω (*sunecho*): to be pressured or to be compelled

5. "shook" — ἐκτινάσσω (*ektinasso*): to shake violently; to wildly swing; to shake until something falls off

6. "I am clean" — **καθαρὸς ἐγώ** (*katharos ego*): the word **καθαρὸς** (*katharos*) means cleansed or pure; **ἐγώ** (*ego*) means "I"; compounded, the phrase is used here to mean, "I have finally gotten you out of my system"; "I am free of you; of your contamination"

7. "henceforth" — **ἀπὸ τοῦ νῦν** (*apo tou nun*): **ἀπὸ** (*apo*) implies a decisive separation; combined, these words mean from this moment or from this exact moment onward

8. "departed" — **μεταβαίνω** (*metabaino*): to step away from; to move into transition; to remove oneself

9. "the Corinthians" — not the Jewish community, but the pagans of the city

10. "be not afraid" — **μή φοβοῦ** (*me phobou*): the word **μὴ** (*me*) is a negative or prohibition; the word **φόβος** (*phobos*) depicts fear, terror, or alarm that results from a threatening or alarming circumstance; as a prohibition, it means put a halt to fear, or it is a command to abruptly stop fearing

11. "speak" — **λαλέω** (*laleo*): to speak; to converse; tense means to keep on talking or speaking

12. "hold not thy peace" — **μὴ σιωπήσῃς** (*me siopeses*) the word **μὴ** (*me*) is a negative or prohibition; the word **σιωπάω** (*siopao*) depicts silence or a hush; as a prohibition, it means put a halt to silence, or it is a command to abruptly stop being quiet

13. "set on" — **ἐπιτίθημι** (*epitithemi*): to set or place a hand on; in this verse, no one will touch you

14. "hurt" — **κακόω** (*kakoo*): to injure, harm, or maltreat; pictures injustice

15. "drave" — **ἀπελαύνω** (*apelauno*): to drive away, like a wind that drives away dust

16. "the Greeks" — **Ἕλλην** (*Hellen*): Greek; in context, pagans who had accepted Christ

17. "beat" — **τύπτω** (*tupto*): pictures a serious beating

18. "cared" — **μέλει** (*melei*): anxious, concerned, interested, thoughtful; he wasn't the least bit interested

SYNOPSIS

There is a sweet satisfaction of knowing you are where God wants you to be, doing what He has called you to do. In fact, when you are obediently functioning in His will, you are very pleasing to Him. And the Bible says, "When a man's ways please the Lord, he maketh even his enemies to be at peace with him" (Proverbs 16:7).

The apostle Paul experienced this firsthand. After several years of struggling to reach the Jews with the Gospel, he finally got into his God-assigned place as an apostle to the Gentiles and began to experience the power and provision of God like never before. Even when the Jews in the city of Corinth violently rose up and tried to stop him from teaching, God gave him favor with the Roman governor and supernaturally protected him from all harm.

The emphasis of this lesson:

Like the apostle Paul, when you finally get into your God-assigned place where you are called to be, a special level of supernatural protection, provision, and power will come to you. He will make even your enemies to be at peace with you.

Out of Disaster, God Forged a Divine Connection

The Bible says, "After these things Paul departed from Athens, and came to Corinth; and found a certain Jew named Aquila, born in Pontus, lately come from Italy, with his wife Priscilla; (because that Claudius had commanded all Jews to depart from Rome:) and came unto them" (Acts 18:1,2).

We know from one early Roman historian named Suetonius that the reigning Emperor Claudius had displaced Jews who "were constantly inciting tumults under their leader Christos." They were creating such a disturbance in the Jewish neighborhoods in Rome that Claudius evicted them from the city. This was an enormous loss for Aquila and Priscilla financially, mentally, emotionally, and socially. From their home in Rome, they headed for the nearest port, where they boarded a ship and began traveling east — not by choice, but rather by force. Ultimately that ship would take them to Corinth.

When Aquila and Priscilla finally arrived in Corinth, they disembarked feeling dejected and defeated. The Bible says they had "lately come from Italy." The words "lately come" in Greek describe *fresh meat that had just been butchered*. The use of these words indicates that Aquila and Priscilla had just *freshly arrived* off the ship from Rome in that very moment.

Meanwhile, feeling despondent and discouraged, Paul was entering Corinth from the east after having left Athens. As the three walked the streets of the unfamiliar, pagan city, they just "happened" to meet up with each other. The Bible says Paul "found" Aquila and Priscilla. We saw that the word "found" is the Greek word *heurisko*, which denotes *a moment when one makes a surprising discovery*. It is from where we get the word "eureka." The moment these three stumbled upon one another, it was truly a "eureka" moment.

What the enemy had meant for evil, God turned into something good! Indeed, "We know that all things work together for good to them that love God, to them who are called according to his purpose" (Romans 8:28). Although God did not cause Aquila and Priscilla to be evicted from Rome and lose all that they had, He used the situation to connect them with the apostle Paul and forge one of the greatest ministry teams of all time.

Why Was Paul 'Pressed' When Silas and Timothy Arrived?

The Bible says as soon as Paul made it to Corinth, "...he reasoned in the synagogue every sabbath, and persuaded the Jews and the Greeks" (Acts 18:4). Not only was he reasoning and persuading the Jews — those who were Jewish by birth and by faith — he was also reasoning and persuading "the Greeks." The phrase "the Greeks" is the word *Hellen*, and it means *Greek*; *non-Jewish*; *gentile*; or *pagan*. Thus, Paul had expanded his sphere of influence to embrace the people Christ had called him to reach, and he was finally beginning to have some measurable success.

But then something unexpected happened. Acts 18:5 says, "And when Silas and Timotheus were come from Macedonia, Paul was pressed in the spirit, and testified to the Jews that Jesus was Christ." Prior to this time, Silas and Timothy had traveled with Paul for years and watched him minister only to Jews. In fact, in every city they went, they watched Paul immediately make a dash for the synagogue to reason with the Jews. For him to now totally focus on sharing the Gospel with the Gentiles was quite a shock.

The *King James Version* of this verse says, "...Paul was pressed in the spirit...." However, in the original Greek text, the words "in the spirit" do *not* appear in the most ancient manuscripts. It simply says, "…Paul was pressed.…"

The word "pressed" is the Greek word *sunecho*, which means *to be pressured* or *to be compelled*; it carries the idea of *manipulation*. Up until that point, Paul and Aquila and Priscilla had been presenting the Gospel to Gentiles and Jews alike and having great success among the Gentiles. But when Silas and Timothy showed up, Paul felt "pressed" — *pressured, compelled, manipulated* — to go back to his old way of doing things, which was speaking to Jews only.

It seems that the moment Silas and Timothy arrived they must have put pressure on Paul. Maybe they went to him and said, "What are you doing? Have you forgotten that you're a Jew? Have you forgotten the Gospel is to the Jew first? Why are you spending all your time and energy speaking to these Greek pagans? What has happened to you?"

Paul Made a Clean Break from Pursuing the Jews

When Paul felt pressed and turned his attention entirely back to the Jews, the Bible says the Jews "…opposed themselves, and blasphemed, [and] he [Paul] shook his raiment, and said unto them, Your blood be upon your own heads; I am clean: from henceforth I will go unto the Gentiles" (Acts 18:6).

The moment Paul turned his attention back to the Jews, they became hostile and began to use profane, blasphemous language and attack him with derogatory, defaming words against his character. When he saw their reaction, he instantly "shook his raiment." The word "shook" in Greek is *ektinasso*, which means *to shake violently; to wildly swing; to shake until something falls off*. Paul's response was in obedience to what Jesus Himself said in the gospels: "And whosoever shall not receive you, nor hear your words, when ye depart out of that house or city, shake off the dust of your feet" (Matthew 10:14).

Paul's actions were an indictment against the Jewish community for not listening to and receiving the message of truth that would save them and transform their lives. He went on to say, "…Your blood be upon your own heads; I am clean…" (Acts 18:6). The phrase "I am clean" in Greek is *katharos ego*. The word *ego* means "I" and denotes Paul *emphatically drawing attention to himself*, and the word *katharos* means *cleansed or pure*. When *katharos ego* are joined together, it is the equivalent of Paul saying,

"I have finally gotten you out of my system; I am free of you — of your contamination."

After years of painstaking efforts to reach the Jews and being brutally mistreated in return, Paul finally reached a breaking point where he had had enough. Accordingly, he said, "…From henceforth I will go unto the Gentiles" (Acts 18:6). The word "henceforth" in Greek is *apo tou nun*. The word *apo* denotes a *decisive separation*. Essentially, Paul declared *from that exact moment forward*, he would separate himself from his past activities and redirect his efforts toward the Gentiles.

There Was an Immediate Harvest of Souls

Scripture goes on to say, "And he departed thence, and entered into a certain man's house, named Justus, one that worshipped God, whose house joined hard to the synagogue" (Acts 18:7). The word "departed" here is the Greek word *metabaino*, which means *to step away from; to remove oneself;* or *to move into transition*. Paul was *transitioning* from his previous fruitless ministry to the Jews into his God-ordained ministry to the Gentiles.

Immediately, positive changes began to occur. Acts 18:8 says, "And Crispus, the chief ruler of the synagogue, believed on the Lord with all his house; and many of the Corinthians hearing believed, and were baptized." The moment Paul made the decision to redirect his energy and efforts to the Gentiles, Crispus and his whole household got saved. This man was the *chief ruler* or *chief rabbi* who was responsible for all worship and activities that took place in the synagogue.

Upon hearing this news of Crispus' salvation, the Bible says "…many of the Corinthians believed and were baptized." The phrase "the Corinthians" does not refer to the Jewish community, but to *the pagans* of the city. Thus, when Paul got his priorities straight and began reaching out to the Gentiles Christ had called him to reach, a multitude in the city believed and were baptized.

This was only the beginning of what God did. The Bible states that "…signs, and wonders, and mighty deeds" were done in Corinth through the apostle Paul (2 Corinthians 12:12). Phenomenal power was unleashed when he got into alignment with God's plan for his life. Likewise, when you align yourself with God's will for your life, you can expect His divine power, provision, and protection to come to your life too.

God Promised To Be With Paul and Protect Him

Immediately after the multitude of Corinthians got saved, the Bible says, "Then spake the Lord to Paul in the night by a vision, Be not afraid, but speak, and hold not thy peace" (Acts 18:9).

The words "Be not afraid" in Greek are *me phobou*. The word *me* is *a negative* or *prohibition*; the word *phobos* depicts *fear, terror, or alarm that results from a threatening or alarming circumstance*. It is from where we get the word "phobia." When the Lord spoke this prohibition to Paul, He was telling him, "Put a halt to fear! Stop it and stop it now!" This was *a command to abruptly stop fearing*.

Furthermore, the Lord said, "...but speak, and hold not thy peace." The word "speak" is the Greek word *laleo*, which means *to speak* or *to converse*. The tense here means *to keep on talking* or *keep on speaking*. The phrase "hold not thy peace" in Greek is again *a negative* or a *prohibition* that literally means *put a halt to silence*; it is *a command to abruptly stop being quiet*. The use of these words lets us know that Paul was being tempted to be silent because of some type of fear. But God commanded him, "Put a halt to fear. Speak now and put an end to your silence!"

With this directive, God promised, "For I am with thee, and no man shall set on thee to hurt thee: for I have much people in this city" (Acts 18:10). Wow! What encouraging news — not just for Paul, but for us also. When we are in the right, God-assigned place, doing the right thing, He promises to be with us and protect us!

The phrase "set on" in Greek is *epitithemi*, which means *to set or place a hand on*. In this verse, it specifically means *no one will touch you*. God said, "...no man shall set on thee to hurt thee...." The word "hurt" is the Greek word *kakao*, which means *to injure, harm, or maltreat*; it depicts *injustice*. It's important to notice that God didn't say people wouldn't try to lay a hand on Paul — He just said none of their efforts would be effective.

The Enemy's Attempted Plot Was Neutralized

The Bible goes on to say that Paul "...continued there a year and six months, teaching the word of God among them" (Acts 18:11). For the first time ever, we see that Paul experienced uninterrupted ministry opportunities among the people for a span of 18 months — then the devil attacked. Verse 12 says, "And when Gallio was the deputy of Achaia, the

Jews made insurrection with one accord against Paul, and brought him to the judgment seat."

Gallio was serving as the "deputy," which means he was the *pro-counselor* or *governor*, and on that particular day he was seated at the judgment seat. The word "judgment" in Greek is *bema*, and it describes *the platform on which judges sat to give out punishments or rewards.* The irate Jews brought Paul to Gallio with the desire of him being judged and sentenced. They claimed, "…This fellow persuadeth men to worship God contrary to the law" (Acts 18:13).

Obviously, Paul was no stranger to this type of opposition. Scripture reveals he had experienced situations like this on multiple occasions. This time, however, something was different. The Bible says, "And when Paul was now about to open his mouth, Gallio said unto the Jews, If it were a matter of wrong or wicked lewdness, O ye Jews, reason would that I should bear with you: But if it be a question of words and names, and of your law, look ye to it; for I will be no judge of such matters. And he drave them from the judgment seat" (Acts 18:14-16).

The word "drave" in verse 16 is the Greek word *apelauno*, which means *to drive away, like a wind that drives away dust.* This tells us that the Jews were so dissatisfied with Gallio's decision they continued to linger around, trying to get him to change his mind. When Gallio saw that they weren't going to leave, he forcefully drove them away from his judgment seat.

Acts 18:17 says, "Then all the Greeks took Sosthenes, the chief ruler of the synagogue, and beat him before the judgment seat. And Gallio cared for none of those things." Interestingly, the phrase "the Greeks" here describes *the pagans who had accepted Christ.* These recent Gentile converts grabbed hold of Sosthenes, the chief ruler of the synagogue, and beat him in front of the governor.

The word "beat" is the Greek word *tupto*, which describes *a serious beating.* Yet, regardless of the severity of the beating, "…Gallio cared for none of those things." The word "cared" in Greek is *melei*, which means *anxious, concerned, interested, or thoughtful.* In this case, it means Gallio *wasn't the least bit interested* in what they were doing.

We Can Experience Peace — Even With Our Enemies

The Scripture goes on to say, "And Paul after this tarried there yet a good while, and then took his leave of the brethren, and sailed thence into Syria, and with him Priscilla and Aquila…" (Acts 18:18). So in addition to the year and a half of unopposed ministry, Paul had even more uninterrupted time to teach the Scriptures and advance God's Kingdom in the city of Corinth.

Remember Sosthenes, the chief ruler of the synagogue who was severely beaten in front of Gallio's judgment seat? Paul mentions him again in First Corinthians 1:1 saying, "Paul, called to be an apostle of Jesus Christ through the will of God, and Sosthenes our brother." The same man who previously brought charges against Paul was now Paul's ministry companion! Somehow, through all that had transpired, God saved this man.

This clearly demonstrates God's promise found in Proverbs 16:7: "When a man's ways please the Lord, he maketh even his enemies to be at peace with him." Friend, if you will get in God's assigned place for you, you will find a new measure of protection, power, and peace on display in your life!

STUDY QUESTIONS

> Study to shew thyself approved unto God, a workman that needeth
> not to be ashamed, rightly dividing the word of truth.
> — 2 Timothy 2:15

1. Proverbs 16:7 says, "When a man's ways please the Lord, he maketh even his enemies to be at peace with him." This promise of divine protection is all through Scripture. Take time to carefully meditate on these promises and ask the Holy Spirit to give you a heart revelation of this truth.
   - **Hebrews 13:5,6**
   - **Psalm 34:7**
   - **Psalm 41:1-3**
   - **Psalm 121**
   - **Psalm 125:2**

PRACTICAL APPLICATION

But be ye doers of the word, and not hearers only,
deceiving your own selves.
—James 1:22

1. When Paul turned back to pursuing the Jews and they retaliated with more hostility and blasphemy, he had a "come to Jesus" moment. From that point forward, he made a clean break with his past activities and focused on what God had called him to do. Are you at a breaking point in your life? Is there anything you're doing that consistently yields *frustration* and ignites *hostility*? What is God showing you to make a clean break from?

2. God told Paul, "Be not afraid," which means *"Put a halt to fear!"* What fearful, threatening or alarming circumstance are you facing in your life? Stop and pray right now, asking God for His grace, which is His power (*see* James 4:6), to be bold as a lion (*see* Proverbs 28:1) and put a stop to fear.

LESSON 4

TOPIC

Embracing Your God-Given Place

SCRIPTURES

1. **1 Corinthians 1:10-13** — Now I beseech you, brethren, by the name of our Lord Jesus Christ, that ye all speak the same thing, and that there be no divisions among you; but that ye be perfectly joined together in the same mind and in the same judgment. For it hath been declared unto me of you, my brethren, by them which are of the house of Chloe, that there are contentions among you. Now this I say, that every one of you saith, I am of Paul; and I of Apollos; and I of Cephas; and I of Christ. Is Christ divided...

2. **1 Corinthians 3:1-10** — And I, brethren, could not speak unto you as unto spiritual, but as unto carnal, even as unto babes in Christ. I have fed you with milk, and not with meat: for hitherto ye were not able to bear it, neither yet now are ye able. For ye are yet carnal: for

whereas there is among you envying, and strife, and divisions, are ye not carnal, and walk as men? For while one saith, I am of Paul; and another, I am of Apollos; are ye not carnal? Who then is Paul, and who is Apollos, but ministers by whom ye believed, even as the Lord gave to every man? I have planted, Apollos watered; but God gave the increase. So then neither is he that planteth any thing, neither he that watereth; but God that giveth the increase. Now he that planteth and he that watereth are one: and every man shall receive his own reward according to his own labour. For we are labourers together with God: ye are God's husbandry, ye are God's building. According to the grace of God which is given unto me, as a wise masterbuilder, I have laid the foundation, and another buildeth thereon. But let every man take heed how he buildeth thereupon.

GREEK WORDS

1. "divisions" — **σχίσμα** (*schisma*): to tear apart, as in violently rending or shredding a garment to pieces; to spilt; it's where we get the word "schism"

2. "joined together" — **καταρτίζω** (*kataridzo*): to put back into order; to mend; to repair; used to depict the restoration of order after a civil war

3. "contentions" — **ἔρις** (*eris*): used in a political context to describe political parties that had different platforms or agendas; some newer translations translate it as a party spirit; a bitterly competitive spirit so consumed with its own self-interests and self-ambitions that it is even willing to split and divide to achieve its own goals and purposes

4. "every one" — **ἕκαστος** (*hekastos*): an all-inclusive term that embraces everyone, with no one excluded

5. "divided" — **μερίζω** (*meridzo*): to divide; to divide into parts; to cut into pieces; to shred

6. "carnal" — **σαρκικός** (*sarkikos*): fleshly; given to fleshly behavior; carnal

7. "envying" — **ζῆλος** (*zelos*): in a negative sense, depicts a self-consumed person who is driven to see his agenda adopted; one who is competitive; could denote one upset because someone else achieved more or received more; one jealous, envious, resentful, and filled with ill will for the one who got what he wanted; fierce competitiveness

8. "strife" — **ἐριθεία** (*eritheia*): a political party; often translated as a party spirit because of its connection to political systems and politi-

cal parties; pictures an individual or group of people who push their agenda and ideas, fighting fiercely to see their platform accepted; thus, strife; a self-seeking ambition that is more concerned about itself and the fulfillment of its own wants, desires, and pleasures than it is in meeting needs in others

9. "by whom" — δι' ὧν (*di' on*): indicates instrumentality; in context, instruments through whom

10. "I planted" — ἐγὼ ἐφύτευσα (*ego ephuteusa*): ἐγὼ (*ego*) means "I," and Paul used it to draw attention to himself; φυτεύω (*phuteuo*) is a root word that means to plant, as a farmer who tills the soil in order to plant seed; Paul said, "I am the one who first tilled the soil and planted the initial seed"

11. "watered" — ποτίζω (*potidzo*): to water, irrigate, or nourish

12. "increase" — αὐξάνω (*auxano*): something amplified, augmented, enlarged, or enhanced; carries the idea of something that escalates and multiplies

13. "anything" — τι (*ti*): depicts the most minute, minuscule object

14. "husbandry" — γεώργιον (*georgian*): field; garden; cultivated field

15. "building" — οἰκοδομή (*oidokome*): construction; conveys the ideas of every facet of building; a building project

16. "according to" — κατά (*kata*): according to; carries the idea of a dominating force

17. "wise" — σοφός (*sophos*): depicts wisdom not naturally attained; special insight

18. "masterbuilder" — ἀρχιτέκτων (*architekton*): architect; one who sees the vision, designs the plan, and oversees construction with others who do the actual building; here, Paul described the leading position of apostolic work, which must be done cooperatively with those gifted in other ways

SYNOPSIS

In his first letter to the church of Corinth, Paul told believers, "According to the grace of God which is given unto me, as a wise masterbuilder, I have laid the foundation…" (1 Corinthians 3:10). When Paul said, "According to the grace of God," he used the Greek word *kata*, which means *to be dominated by*. Thus, Paul was literally saying, "According to the grace of God dominating my life, I have laid the foundation."

From the moment Paul was saved, Jesus called him to be an apostle to the Gentiles. And while he initially struggled to accept his God-assigned place, he eventually reached the point where he raised his white flag and surrendered to God's will for his life. Not only did he embrace his place, but also the grace God had assigned to him. Have you surrendered to God's will for your life? Have you embraced your God-assigned place? Are you receiving His grace to fulfill your assignment?

The emphasis of this lesson:

When you fully embrace your God-assigned place, His special grace will begin to flow to you and through you like a mighty river, dominating your life.

Thus far, we have been looking at the apostle Paul and how it took him some time to transition into his God-assigned place as an apostle to the Gentiles. For the first five years of his ministry, he had reversed God's order of priorities in his life and kept reaching out to the Jews. Finally, when he reached the city of Corinth, that all changed, and he began to experience a highly successful season of ministry to the Gentiles.

Because Paul was an apostle, he eventually moved on from Corinth and went to plant a church in another area — the city of Ephesus. After he had left, he later wrote to the church of Corinth and gave them some very important instructions about embracing their God-assigned place and the specific grace He provides to fulfill their calling.

The Church Was War-Torn

Turning our attention to Paul's first letter to the Corinthians, we see in the first chapter that he is addressing a major problem in the church. It seems that many people were comparing themselves with others in the church, and it was creating quite an upheaval. Paul said,

> **Now I beseech you, brethren, by the name of our Lord Jesus Christ, that ye all speak the same thing, and that there be no divisions among you; but that ye be perfectly joined together in the same mind and in the same judgment (1 Corinthians 1:10).**

One of the first directives Paul gave was that there be no "divisions." This is the Greek word *schism*, which means *to tear apart, as in violently rending or shredding a garment into pieces*. It can also mean *to split* and is from where we get the word *schism*. The use of this word by Paul tells us that the church in Corinth was being ripped into pieces.

Therefore, Paul charged them to be "perfectly joined together." The meaning of these words in Greek is extremely important, because it indicates just how ripped apart the church had become. The phrase "perfectly joined together" is a translation of *kataridzo*, a very old Greek word that was used to depict *the restoration of order after a civil war*. It means *to put back into order; to mend; to repair*.

This lets us know that the damage inside the church of Corinth was equivalent to the devastation left behind by a civil war. People had chosen sides — brother had been fighting against brother — leaving the spiritual landscape littered with casualties. Paul urged the Corinthian believers to put aside their differences, set down their weapons, and restore their relationships by rebuilding their lines of communication.

The Source of the Civil War Within

Why was there so much divisiveness and fighting in the church? Paul revealed the answer in the next verse:

> **For it hath been declared unto me of you, my brethren, by them which are of the house of Chloe, that there are contentions among you (1 Corinthians 1:11).**

The word "contentions" here is a translation of the Greek word *eris*, which is used in a political context to describe *political parties that had different platforms or agendas*. Some newer Bible translations translate the word "contentions" as a "party spirit." This word *eris* denotes *a bitterly competitive spirit so consumed with its own self-interests and self-ambitions that it is even willing to split and divide to achieve its own goals and purposes*.

In the church of Corinth there were different factions, or groups, that were warring against each other. Each church group had its own platform, and just like political parties today, each group was fiercely promoting its own agenda. Who were these factions, or parties, in the church? Paul tells us clearly in verse 12:

> **Now this I say, that every one of you saith, I am of Paul; and I of Apollos; and I of Cephas; and I of Christ (1 Corinthians 1:12).**

The words "every one" is the Greek word *hekastos*, which is *an all-inclusive term that embraces everyone, with no one excluded.* This means the effects of division were affecting every single person in the church. Some people were saying, "I belong to the Paul party." Others said, "I'm in Apollos' camp." Then there were those who claimed to be in Peter's group (who was Cephas), and still others who said they were "of Christ."

Obviously, Paul was the founding pastor of the church in Corinth. Hence, those who said they were in his party had a special love and loyalty to him for all his hard labor. These folks were accustomed to Paul's style and personality. In their minds and hearts, he was the perfect pastor and the only pastor they had ever known.

After Paul left Corinth, Apollos came and began ministering, and his personality and style were quite different. Although Paul was rough and crude in speech, Apollos was very educated and intellectual in his delivery. He became known as the "golden-tongued" orator. With his arrival, a new group emerged in the church that gravitated toward him. Hence a divisive chasm began forming over personality.

It appears that at some point the apostle Peter visited the church of Corinth, giving birth to a third group of people who preferred *his* personality and unique style. Add to these three, a fourth group — the Jesus group. More than likely, these individuals were the "super spiritual" people in the crowd who were loyal only to Christ. Thus, they likely had a difficult time submitting to authority.

To all four of these groups, Paul asked, "Is Christ divided?" (1 Corinthians 1:13). The word "divided" here is the Greek word *meridzo*, which means *to divide; to divide into parts; to cut into pieces; to shred.* This word was used to describe *the violent ripping and tearing of a garment.* Indeed, with four major parties in the church all jockeying for power and fiercely promoting their own agenda, the church of Corinth had become shredded and war-torn.

Envy and Strife Indicate Carnal, Immature Christians

The presence of division and strife in the church was a clear indication of immaturity, which helps us understand why Paul said what he said in First Corinthians 3:1-3:

And I, brethren, could not speak unto you as unto spiritual, but as unto carnal, even as unto babes in Christ. I have fed you with milk, and not with meat: for hitherto ye were not able to bear it, neither yet now are ye able. For ye are yet carnal: for whereas there is among you envying, and strife, and divisions, are ye not carnal, and walk as men?

Notice the word "carnal" used three times in these three verses. It is the Greek word *sarkikos*, which means *fleshly; given to fleshly behavior; carnal.* The majority of believers in Corinth were exhibiting fleshly, un-Christ-like behavior. Specifically, Paul noted "envying and strife."

The word "envying" is from the Greek word *zelos*, which in a negative sense, depicts *a self-consumed person who is driven to see his agenda adopted; one who is competitive.* This word could also denote *one upset because someone else achieved more or received more; one jealous, envious, resentful, and filled with ill will for the one who got what he wanted.* It is *fierce competitiveness.* This is how the Christians in Corinth were acting.

They were also in "strife," which in Greek is the word *eritheia* and describes *a political party.* It is often translated as *a party spirit* because of its connection to political systems and political parties. It pictures *an individual or group of people who push their agenda and ideas, fighting fiercely to see their platform accepted.* Thus, it results in *strife — a self-seeking ambition that is more concerned about itself and the fulfillment of its own wants, desires, and pleasures than it is in meeting needs in others.*

The apostle Paul continued in First Corinthians 3:4 and 5 saying:

For while one saith, I am of Paul; and another, I am of Apollos; are ye not carnal? Who then is Paul, and who is Apollos, but ministers by whom ye believed, even as the Lord gave to every man?

Again, we see Paul call the believers "carnal" — the Greek word *sarkikos*, meaning *fleshly* or *given to fleshly behavior.* He then said something quite unique. He called himself and Apollos ministers "by whom" the people came to believe in Jesus. The words "by whom" in Greek is *di' on*, which indicates *instrumentality.* Hence, Paul is declaring himself (and Apollos) to merely be *instruments through whom* the Holy Spirit chose to work.

If Paul would have been fleshly and competitive, he would have likely said, "Have you forgotten who started this church? I'm the one who painstakingly laid the foundation here. I'm the one who fought the spiritual battles and endured the enemy's assaults to see this church become what it is today — not Apollos." Yet, Paul said *none* of these things. Instead he said, "Who is Paul? What's the big deal about me? Who is Apollos? We're just instruments. Everyone comes to Christ through someone. Don't split the church over this issue."

Only God Can Give the 'Increase'

In Paul's next breath, he said:

> **I have planted, Apollos watered; but God gave the increase (1 Corinthians 3:6).**

The words "I planted" are a translation of the Greek words *ego ephuteusa*. The word *ego* means *I*, and Paul used it to draw attention to himself. The word *phuteuo* means *to plant, as a farmer who tills the soil in order to plant seed*.

Basically, Paul said, "I'm the one who first tilled the soil and planted the initial seed. That was my job. When I finished, someone else came along and watered the seed. That was Apollos." The word "watered" is the Greek word *potidzo*, which means *to water, irrigate, or nourish*. Paul planted and Apollos watered. Both people were needed; neither could have been effective without the other.

Ultimately, Paul said, "…God gave the increase" (1 Corinthians 3:6). In Greek, the word "increase" is *auxano*, which describes *something amplified, augmented, enlarged, or enhanced*. It carries the idea of *something that escalates and multiplies*. Here, Paul refocuses the attention on the most important factor in the equation — *God*. Without Him, we have nothing.

To make sure we get this all-important point, Paul added, "So then neither is he that planteth any thing, neither he that watereth; but God that giveth the increase" (1 Corinthians 3:7). The word "anything" is the Greek word *ti*, and it depicts *the most minute, minuscule object*. Hence, Paul was saying, "Quit thinking about me and Apollos. We're the smallest, most minuscule part of God's immense plan."

The truth is, you can plant seeds of truth, and someone else can come along and water them. But if God doesn't get involved in the process, nothing is going to happen. There is only one Creator of life, and that is God. Paul was trying to shake the Corinthian believers back into reality, urging them to place their eyes back on God instead of human personalities.

In First Corinthians 3:8, Paul went on to say, "Now he that planteth and he that watereth are one: and every man shall receive his own reward according to his own labour." Here he points out that the one who plants and the one who waters have equal importance and value. Although our roles may be different, both are vital in God's plan. And each person will be rewarded individually based upon the merits of his or her own labor.

Paul then added, "For we are labourers together with God: ye are God's husbandry, ye are God's building" (1 Corinthians 3:9). The word "we" refers to Apollos and Paul as partners. The word "together" indicates that Apollos and Paul were working with each other, not against each other. They were working as a team with God, and the believers were His "husbandry," which in Greek is the word *georgian*, and it describes *a field*; *garden*; or *cultivated field*.

Operate in Your God-Given Place Using Your God-Given Grace

It is interesting to note that at this point in the chapter, Paul switched illustrations from farming imagery to construction. Not only are God's people a *cultivated field*, but they are also His "building." The word "building" in verse 9 is the Greek word *oidokome*, which conveys *the ideas of every facet of building*. It can also be translated as *a building project*.

Then Paul said, "According to the grace of God which is given unto me, as a wise masterbuilder, I have laid the foundation, and another buildeth thereon. But let every man take heed how he buildeth thereupon" (1 Corinthians 3:10). The opening phrase "according to" is the Greek word *kata*, which means *according to*, and it carries the idea of *a dominating force*.

Essentially, Paul stated, "I have a special grace that has been given to me by God and it dominates my life, enabling me to do what I am doing. The grace He has given me is uniquely different than what others have been given. I know what my role is, and I am graced for that role."

What was Paul's unique role? He said he was a "wise masterbuilder." The word "wise" in Greek is *sophos*, and it depicts *wisdom not naturally attained; special insight.* And the word "masterbuilder" is the Greek word *architekton*, which describes an *architect; one who sees the vision, designs the plan, and oversees construction with others who do the actual building.* Here, Paul describes the leading position of apostolic work, which must be done in cooperation with those gifted in other ways. He knew his role was an architect and that he was graced for that position. Likewise, he knew he couldn't do anything on his own. He needed the help of others.

The bottom line is, Paul was not threatened by Apollos or by Peter, nor was he competing with them. His role was to be the architect, and that is what he was uniquely graced by God to do. He knew others — like Apollos — were needed to come along after him and build on what he started.

Like Paul, you need to understand what your God-assigned place is and embrace His grace for that role. Don't be afraid that you are less than others, or arrogantly think you are better than others. Don't compare or compete; simply be the best you can be where God has called you. And learn to appreciate the place and purpose He has given others.

STUDY QUESTIONS

Study to shew thyself approved unto God, a workman that needeth not to be ashamed, rightly dividing the word of truth.
— 2 Timothy 2:15

1. Just how effective is your human skill, ingenuity, and efforts apart from God's involvement? He gives us a clear answer in the following passages. Take a few moments to reflect on these truths and write what the Holy Spirit shows you.
   - **John 6:63 and 15:5**
   - **Romans 7:18**
   - **2 Corinthians 3:5**
   - **Psalm 127:1**
   - **Zechariah 4:6**

2. Go back and reread the definitions of "envying" and "strife." Do these traits sound familiar? Instead of chasing selfish ambition, how does God's Word say we should act? (*See* Romans 12:3; Philippians 2:3,4; James 3:14-17; 1 Corinthians 10:24).

3. Clearly, Paul was encouraging all believers to seek peace with each other. What do these verses say to you about *pursuing* and *maintaining peace* with others?
   - **Romans 12:18; 14:19**
   - **Hebrews 12:14,15**
   - **James 3:17,18**

PRACTICAL APPLICATION

> But be ye doers of the word, and not hearers only,
> deceiving your own selves.
> —James 1:22

1. The church of Corinth was deeply divided — so much so that the relational damage was equivalent to the devastation left behind by a civil war. Have you been in a war with another believer? If so, what were you fighting over? How does this lesson help you see things in a different light and challenge you to come up higher?
2. Have you surrendered to God's will for your life? Have you embraced your place and are you receiving His grace to fulfill your assignment?

LESSON 5

TOPIC

Be the Best You Can Be at Whatever God Has Called You To Do

SCRIPTURES

1. **1 Peter 4:10,11** — As every man hath received the gift, even so minister the same one to another, as good stewards of the manifold grace of God. If any man speak, let him speak as the oracles of God; if any man minister, let him do it as of the ability which God giveth: that God in all things may be glorified through Jesus Christ, to whom be praise and dominion for ever and ever. Amen.

GREEK WORDS

1. "every man" — ἕκαστος (*hekastos*): an all-inclusive term that embraces everyone, with no one excluded

2. "received" — λαμβάνω (*lambano*): to receive into one's possession; to take into one's own control and ownership; carries the idea of taking hold of something, grasping onto something, and embracing it so tightly that it becomes your very own; as used in this verse, it means that God sees it as our responsibility to accept and take ownership of these gifts as our own

3. "gift" — χάρισμα (*charisma*): a grace-given gift; derived from χάρις (*charis*), the word for grace; when it becomes *charisma*, it depicts something that is given or imparted by grace; in history, used to describe that moment when the gods graced or donated supernatural ability, favor, or power to an individual; thus, this word means a gracious gift; a person who has received a *charisma* has received a donation or an enablement from God that equips him in some supernatural manner

4. "minister" — διακονέω (*diakoneo*): a servant whose primary responsibility is to serve food and wait on tables; pictures a waiter who painstakingly attends to the needs and wishes of the patron; this servant's supreme task is to please clients; therefore, he serves honorably, pleasurably, and in a fashion that makes the people he waits on feel as if they are nobility; this is a committed, professional server who is zealously dedicated to doing his job on the highest level possible

5. "good" — καλός (*kalos*): good or useful; can refer to that which is outwardly attractive or to what is inwardly noble; it is frequently used to denote good, noble actions or superior behavior; something that is exceptional, of the highest quality, outstanding, or superb

6. "stewards" — οἰκονόμος (*oikonomos*): portrays the rule or management of a house; depicts leaders so trusted by the king or the state that they were appointed to administrate entire departments or nations; used to describe anyone with managerial responsibilities; the word is used in Romans 16:23 to describe a brother in Corinth named Erastus, who was the chamberlain or city manager of Corinth.

7. "manifold" — ποικίλος (*poikilos*): variegated; multi-colored; diverse; diversified

8. "oracles" — λόγιον (*logion*): a divine oracle; a clear channel for the voice for God

9. "as of [the] ability" — ἐξ ἰσχύος (*hos ex ischuos*): out of the mighty strength

10. "giveth" — χορηγέω (*choregeo*): pictures choreography; an epic chorus; a grand event

SYNOPSIS

God has a divine assignment just for you. No one else can fulfill it, and it's very important. There are people all around you who need the gift He has placed on your life. Therefore, He wants you to do everything you can to develop it fully. He said in His Word, "Whatever your hand finds to do, do it with all your might..." (Ecclesiastes 9:10 *NIV*).

How has the Lord gifted you? Are you being a good steward of the gift with which He has graced you? The apostle Peter said, "As every man hath received the gift, even so minister the same one to another, as good stewards of the manifold grace of God" (1 Peter 4:10). In the very next verse, he identifies what our motivation should be for everything we do: "...that God in all things may be glorified through Jesus Christ, to whom be praise and dominion for ever and ever. Amen" (1Peter 4:11).

The emphasis of this lesson:

Don't compare yourself with others or try to compete with the calling on their lives. Know who God called you to be and what He has graced you to do, and do it to the best of your ability.

Take Ownership of the 'Grace-Gift' God's Given You

In our last lesson, we learned how the apostle Paul was graced by God to be a "wise masterbuilder" of the Church. He was specifically gifted to be a spiritual architect who envisioned and designed a blueprint of what the Church needed to be. In the same way, God has a special gift of grace just for you and a place that is uniquely yours in which you are to serve and shine with God's anointing.

Peter talked about this grace in First Peter 4:10. He said, "As every man hath received the gift, even so minister the same one to another, as good stewards of the manifold grace of God." Notice the words "every man." In Greek, it is the word *hekastos*, which is *an all-inclusive term that embraces everyone, with no one excluded*.

So when Peter says, "every man hath received the gift," he is speaking to every single person in the Church. If you are in the Body of Christ, you are included in this number — you too have "received" a gift. The word "received" is a form of the Greek word *lambano*, which is used 258 times in the New Testament. It means *to receive into one's possession; to take into one's own control and ownership.* It carries the idea of *taking hold of something, grasping onto something, and embracing something so tightly that it becomes your very own.*

In the context of this verse, it means that God sees it as our responsibility to accept and take ownership of the gifts He has placed in our lives and make them our own. For instance, if you know God has gifted you to teach the Word, take ownership of that teaching gift He gave you and develop it. Learn how to put together outlines and communicate principles in such a way that people readily understand what is being taught.

Likewise, if you have the gift of giving, nurture it. Learn to be generous and listen for where God wants you to give. Moreover, if your gift is administration, cultivate it. Learn how to organize, prioritize, and delegate tasks. The bottom line — whatever your gift, make every effort to continue to grow and improve in it so you are as effective as you can possibly be to advance God's Kingdom.

God's Grace Is His Divine Enablement

Looking again at First Peter 4:10, "As every man hath received the gift...." The word "gift" here is the Greek word *charisma*, which means *a grace-given gift.* It is derived from the word *charis*, the word for *grace.* When it becomes *charisma*, it depicts *something that is given or imparted by grace; a gracious gift.* This lets us know we are not talking about natural talent or ability. Yes, God's grace may work through our natural talents, but it is a supernatural endowment and can only be imparted to us by His grace. There is no room for boasting or self-glory in the possession of these magnificent gifts.

What's interesting is that the word *charisma* originally came from the pagan world and was used to describe that moment when the gods graced or donated supernatural ability, favor, or power to an individual. Thus, as a recipient of *charisma* you have received *a donation or an enablement from God that equips you in a supernatural manner.*

Taking this a step further, the root word for *charisma* is *charis*, which by itself is the word "grace." In the ancient world, the word "grace" literally described a special touch from the gods, and when a person received "grace" from the gods, it changed them. In fact, it changed them so radically that the word "grace" in some ancient literature meant being under a divine spell. Under divine grace, a person behaved very differently and was able to do what he or she normally would never be able to do on their own.

Are you seeing the connection? When God touches you with His grace, it's like you come under His divine spell. His grace empowers you and transforms you — it is a divine donation from Heaven that enables you to do what you could never naturally do on your own. The Bible says "every man hath received the gift," which means if Jesus is your Lord and Savior, you have received a *charisma* and the grace of God is operating in your life!

What It Means To 'Minister' Your Gift

Again, Peter said, "As every man hath received the gift, even so minister the same one to another..." (1 Peter 4:10). The word "minister" is a translation of the Greek word *diakoneo*, which describes *a servant whose primary responsibility is to serve food and wait on tables*. It pictures *a waiter who painstakingly attends to the needs and wishes of a patron; this servant's supreme task is to please clients*. Therefore, he serves honorably, pleasurably, and in a fashion that makes the people he waits on feel as if they are nobility. *This is a committed, professional server who is zealously dedicated to doing his job on the highest level possible.*

Peter has told us that every believer in the Church has received a grace-gift. Our part is to *accept the gift* (our God-assigned place) we've been given. Next, we are to *take ownership of the gift*. That is, we are to take the divine donation from Heaven and *develop it* to such an extent that we become excellent and proficient on the highest level possible. We are to function as professional servers who are radically and passionately committed to using our gifts to please God and meet the needs of others.

Notice to whom we are to minister our gifts. The Bible says *to one another*, which means the focus is on others, not ourselves. These gifts are not given for self-glory or self-promotion. We are divinely graced by God with special gifts to be a blessing to others in the Body of Christ. If you will take the gifts God has given you and release them into the lives of others, they will be blessed and so will you!

You Are Called To Be a 'Good Steward'

Next, Peter said we are to minister our gifts "…as good stewards of the manifold grace of God" (1 Peter 4:10). The word "good" is the plural version of the Greek word *kalos*, which means *good or useful*. It can refer to *that which is outwardly attractive, or to what is inwardly noble; it is frequently used to denote good, noble actions, or superior behavior.* Indeed, it is *something that is exceptional, of the highest quality, outstanding, or superb.* This is the kind of "stewards" we are to be.

The word "stewards" is the Greek word *oikonomos*, which describes *the rule or management of a house.* It was used to depict *leaders so trusted by the king or state that they were appointed to administrate entire departments or nations.* Moreover, it described *anyone with managerial responsibilities.* We find this word *oikonomos* used in Romans 16:23 to describe a brother in Corinth named Erastus, who was the "chamberlain" or "city manager" of Corinth.

By using the word *oikonomos*, Peter profoundly declared that when God placed His grace-given gifts inside of us, He was making us stewards of His own personal treasures. Consequently, He expects us to be faithful managers of the gifts He has entrusted to our care. He wants us to use our gifts regularly to meet the needs of those around us and to do it in such a way that He receives all the glory.

Thus, we are to take personal ownership of the supernatural, grace-given gift — the *charisma* — from God and develop it to the highest degree possible. As servants, we are to share our gifts with others with outstanding excellence — like superior, noble managers who have been entrusted with responsibility by the King of kings and Lord of lords. What an amazing privilege we've been given!

God's Grace Is 'Manifold'

Furthermore, the Bible says we are to be "…good stewards of the manifold grace of God" (1 Peter 4:10). The word "manifold" here is the Greek word *poikilos*. It is the same word used in the Septuagint, which is the Greek version of the Old Testament, to describe Joseph's coat of many colors (*see* Genesis 37:3). The word *poikilos* means *variegated; multi-colored; diverse; diversified.*

A great example of the word "manifold" (*poikilos*) is demonstrated in the multiple facets of a diamond. When you place a diamond in the light, each angled surface begins to refract the light brilliantly with different colors. It is dazzling to see. In the same way, the grace of God has been placed in us in such a way that we each reflect the light of His glory in our own unique way.

Our differences are what make the body of Christ so interesting! Being different is not bad — *it's good*. It displays the manifold grace of God working in us. It is multicolored, diverse, and beautiful! Why would you want to be like someone else when you can be who you are? God wants you to shine your own brilliant color and dazzle in a way that is different than everyone else!

Putting the meanings of all these words together, here is the *Renner Interpretive Version (RIV)* of First Peter 4:10:

> **Every single one of you, without exception, has received a grace-given gift. Embrace what God has placed inside you. Take ownership of it and do your best to develop and use that gift to meet the needs of one another. God has entrusted a great deal to you by placing such a dazzling gift in your life, and He is depending on you to be faithful with this important responsibility.**

The Manifestation of God's Grace-Gifts Is Like a Choreographed Event for All To See

Peter went on to say, "If any man speak, let him speak as the oracles of God; if any man minister, let him do it as of the ability which God giveth: that God in all things may be glorified through Jesus Christ, to whom be praise and dominion for ever and ever. Amen" (1 Peter 4:11).

The word "oracles" in this verse is the Greek word *logion*, and it describes *a divine oracle* or *a clear channel for the voice for God*. We should do everything we can to be the clearest channel possible for God to speak through. This includes keeping ourselves pure and uncontaminated from the world (*see* James 1:27) and making every effort to set no vile thing before our eyes (*see* Psalm 101:3). As we learn how to take ownership of our grace-given gift, the Holy Spirit will prompt us on what to do to be the clearest channel for God's grace to flow through.

Additionally, the Bible says, "…if any man minister, let him do it as of the ability which God giveth…" (1 Peter 4:11). The phrase "as of the ability" in Greek is *ex ischuos*, which means *out of the mighty strength*. The word "giveth" is the Greek word *choregeo*, which means *choreography*, and it describes *an epic chorus* or *a grand event*. This indicates that when the grace of God operates through God's people, it is quite a production to see! It is like *a theatrical event or spectacle*, with the Holy Spirit taking center stage.

Friend, God wants you to be the best you that you can be — not a cheap imitation of someone else. Quit comparing yourself with others and learn to accept and fully embrace your God-assigned place. Whatever God has gifted and called you to do, do it with all your might! (*See* Ecclesiastes 9:10 *NIV.*)

STUDY QUESTIONS

> Study to shew thyself approved unto God, a workman that needeth
> not to be ashamed, rightly dividing the word of truth.
> — 2 Timothy 2:15

The Bible says we are to be "good stewards" of the grace-gifts God has given us, which means we are to be *faithful servants* who manage well what He has entrusted to us.

1. What is the resounding truth found in Haggai 2:8; Psalm 24:1 and 50:10-12?

2. Carefully read the parable of the talents in Matthew 25:14-30. According to Jesus, how does a "good and faithful servant" operate? How does a "lazy servant" operate, and what is his perspective of Jesus? What does this parable personally speak to you?

3. Paul's message in Ephesians 6:7 and 8 and Colossians 3:22-24 are very similar. What do these passages say to you about your motivation for serving others with your gifts?

PRACTICAL APPLICATION

> But be ye doers of the word, and not hearers only,
> deceiving your own selves.
> — James 1:22

1. Are you aware of the grace-given gifts God has deposited in your life? If so, which ones can you identify? Name at least one gift you have received that energizes you with passion and joy when you have the opportunity to share it with others.

2. Give a brief testimony of how God's divine endowment operates through you to touch other people? How has it made a difference in their lives?

3. What are you doing to cultivate and develop your gifts? How can you better "minister" them to meet the needs of others? What is one practical way you can use your gifts more regularly?

4. What is one grace-gift (*charisma*) that you don't have but greatly appreciate in someone else? How does their gift fill a need in your life?

Notes

www.ingramcontent.com/pod-product-compliance
Lightning Source LLC
Chambersburg PA
CBHW051048030426
42339CB00006B/246